Jacqueline, from
your loving son
David xx
Christmas Day 1987.

Endpapers:
La Place des Amis Réunis

RONALD SEARLE

Ah Yes, I Remember it Well...

PARIS 1961-1975

PAVILION
MICHAEL JOSEPH

This edition first published in Great Britain in 1987 by
Pavilion Books Limited
196 Shaftesbury Avenue, London WC2H 8JL
in association with Michael Joseph Limited
27 Wrights Lane, Kensington, London W8 5TZ

These drawings first appeared in *PARIS! PARIS!*
by Irwin Shaw and Ronald Searle
published by
Harcourt Brace Jovanovich, New York, 1977
Weidenfeld and Nicolson Limited, London, 1977

All the original drawings are in the collection of
Dr André Willemin, Paris

British Library Cataloguing in Publication Data
Searle, Ronald
    Ah yes, I remember it well.
    1. Paris (France)——Social life and customs
    ——20th century——Caricatures and cartoons
    I. Title
    944.360838'0207   DC715

ISBN 1-85145-153-6

Printed and bound in Great Britain

FOR MÔ

M'sieur, when a man is tired of Paris,
he is tired of life, n'est-ce pas?

Dr Johnson (according to certain French sources)

A blindfolded traveller with an approximate sense of smell, parachuted into the Carrefour de l'Odéon at 6.30 am on a dark winter's morning, would know at once that he is not on the Danish pastry side of Madison at 76th, or abandoned in the outer wastes of culinary Kew.

The unique odours of gently stewing coffee, Left Bank sewers, warm *baguettes* in their big baskets and the first Gauloise of the day on the breath of an unshaven smoker, all mingling into a memorable whole, whisper one thing only: 'Paree'.

The smells of central Paris, unlike those of London or New York, are the unmistakable essence of its small and fast disappearing villages. Nostalgia Hall for the tourist breathing them in greedily (knowing he has a return ticket in his pocket); oxygen for that anonymous mass of locals with their crumb-littered shopping bags who scurry out of the chipped and flaking warrens behind the Louis XIV façades at the first clang of an opening protective grill on the nearest shop.

Like the sewer rats, sitting back in the gutter at first light calmly cleaning their whiskers before effacing themselves down the nearest drain, the real Paris becomes fleetingly visible in the early hours of the morning: downing its *petit blanc*, hauling out its overflowing *poubelles*, seeking its ideal *flûtes* and *bâtards*, loading up with thin milk and fat cheeses, grabbing its *Equipe* before being submerged by the 'day' people who grimly flood into town *au job* on rafts of *tartines* through monstrous seas of coffee with chicory extract.

Paris has always been a full to overflowing city and only incidentally a commuter destination. Every centimetre of living and dying space has been occupied uninterruptedly since the days of the Parisii. Behind the rightly famous narrative of sumptuous living lies buried an unwritten story of secret encounters, struggles for survival and anonymous suffering.

Even today, on a more trivial level, anyone who has experienced being hard-up – let alone a state of downright poverty – in a two by three metre *chambre de bonne* on the seventh floor of an architectural jewel with one communal tap out in the corridor, will appreciate that the accomplishment of only token ablutions can be a considerable acrobatic feat, as well as an act of great will-power. Yet Parisians are not dirty. They merely have their own special patina.

Naturally, there is Paris and Paris. Everyone has their own, to the exclusion of anyone else's. Mine has always been closer to the back streets than to the boulevards, and my memory of them remains the wildly rich visual diary of a decade and a half of intimate close-ups: family snaps, rather than cinematic sweeps over grandiose panoramas and decorated *poitrines*.

There have been exceptions, of course. Nothing will ever obliterate the recollection of magical evenings spent sitting on that defaced and battered bench in the middle of the Pont des Arts, feet in the litter, barrel-organ piping away nearby, hypnotised by the multi-layered view of the full span of the Pont Neuf and the Ile de la Cité catching the last light of day and the first floodlights of the night. All that, whilst holding the hand of *the* girl. Then wandering back under the golden dome of the Institut de France, up the Rue Mazarine and past Marcelle's restaurant, across the Carrefour de l'Odéon without getting compressed by the 86 bus, to the Rue Antoine Dubois and so to bed. (Sigh . . .)

The Rue Antoine Dubois, which became my home with Monica (see girl above) for fourteen years from 10 September 1961, is probably the shortest street in Paris. Sandwiched between the Rue de l'Ecole de Médecine and the Rue Monsieur le Prince, it was created in 1672 on what was left of the thirteenth-century Collège des Cordeliers. It is three tall houses long, ending in a bank of steps and a minuscule rubbish-strewn garden in front of which stands an uninspired, usually urine-splashed, life-size statue of the surgeon Alfred Vulpian (nineteenth-century explorer of *'quelques'* nerves of the cranium). At that time it was the HQ of one of the ripest bands of *clochards* this side of Notre Dame. Opposite our windows (first at No. 2 and later at No. 4) were the gloomy laboratories of the bacteriological faculty of the Ecole de Médecine – in whose dissecting department many pickled corpses of these same *clochards* probably ended.

Since 1688, when *A New Description of Paris* was published 'by Henry Bonwicke at the Red Lyon in St. Paul's Church-Yard' ('there being hitherto nothing of this subject in our language'), something like a quarter of a million books have been devoted to this 'Polite and Beautiful City', as well as an awful lot of pictures. So I won't go on except to say that, so far as my own efforts are concerned, the drawings reproduced in this album are virtually the only ones I made of Paris in all the years I lived there. Why? Mainly because I was haunted (as in Venice) by the image of all those unfathomable lakes of paint, that deadly forest of brushes, those great vats of ink, those buckets-full of steely pens, those endlessly sharpened pencils, with which hordes of artists over the centuries have eagerly splashed, scratched, scraped and scribbled over any vista worth a glance, so that I simply did not have the courage to add to the mess.

Nevertheless, ten years ago, these drawings appeared in yet another book about Paris. There they were, over-reduced and in conflict with the text they accompanied. Their reappearance now, alone, in a more generous format will, I hope, justify their existence. They aim to present a view of Paris from the inside as it tottered through the sixties into the seventies via May '68. Those who know Paris intimately will notice at once that certain scenes have been amalgamated into something rather more representative of Paris than is possible for the usual pedestrian snapshots. These drawings attempt to show, in fact, what it *feels* like to live in Paris, rather than what one might imagine it is like. At least, that was the idea . . . .

RONALD SEARLE
Haute Provence,
Spring 1987

En avant! (more or less). Arc de
Triomphe, Place Charles de Gaulle

An interesting, ornate, late seventeenth-century doorway, not too far from Saint Germain des Prés

Somewhere on the Left Bank, heading toward the Institut de France – but rarely getting there

7.30 am, after a swift couple of *petits noirs* well laced with firewater, there are those who swear that the cast-iron foliage of the Hector Guimard métro entrances begins to creep about . . .

Strictly for the birds, in the gardens of the Palais Royal

19

Montparnasse, and Pompidou's Folly

Starkers corner, Rue Saint Honoré

Since the Hunchback, much has been thrown up on the *parvis* of Notre Dame de Paris

Admirers of Mona Lisa Gherardini del
Giocondo disembarking at the Louvre

The French are renowned for their love
of animals

Drowsy afternoon in the Luxembourg Gardens

– ★★★–!!!–★★★!! – et merde, monsieur!

Avenue de l'Opéra, Land of the Rising Yen

Daisies for maman

43

Bonne chance . . .

51

Four knives and forks Michelin

. . . or a little place in the Midi, maybe . . .

More clowns, more wide-eyed children, and more phoneys to the square metre than any other public place in Europe (Saint Tropez compris). La Place du Tertre, Montmartre – artistic rubbish dump of Paris – and two born every minute to keep it thriving

'MACHIN TRUC AU POTEAU!'
Protest march from the Bastille to the
Ministry of Agriculture by the SSBF
(Syndicate of Supporters of Breast
Feeding), to mark their outrage at the
Minister's suggestion that the public
drink more milk and cut down on
the alcohol

Mon appartement, ma terrasse, mon
parasol, mon panorama, mon whisky . . .